MW01114684

Copyright © 2018 by Catherine Adams.
All rights reserved. This book or any portion thereof
may not be reproduced or used in any manner whatsoever without
the express written permission of the publisher.

Father and Daughter Journal

Catherine Adams

How to use this journal

Use the journal in the way that makes the most sense for you and your daughter. If she doesn't like to write, you can read and discuss the questions with her. If she enjoys writing, then you can take turns filling out the pages. If you need more space, there are blank pages at the end of every question and there are additional sheets in the back of the journal.

If there are questions that don't apply or that either of you don't like...skip them! Feel free to jump around or take turns picking questions; there is no specific order to them and no need to do every one.
I sincerely hope that you will be able to discuss your answers with each other, bond, and above all else, have fun!

Your daughter woke up this morning with one of the following traits. Check which you think will be her top two choices:

_____ Amazingly Athletic

_____ Stunningly Beautiful

_____ Crazy Smart

_____ Super Popular

_____ Musically Gifted

What trait would you choose for her? Why?

_____

_____

_____

_____

_____

_____

_____

_____

_____

1

You woke up this morning with one of the following traits. Rank them from 1- 3 which you would want to be:

_____ Amazingly Athletic

_____ Stunningly Beautiful

_____ Crazy Smart

_____ Super Popular

_____ Musically Gifted

How would your life be different if you got your top choice? Which trait do you think your dad would want you to have?

_____

_____

_____

_____

_____

_____

_____

We answer/discuss

After you both have answered, discuss or write why you chose the traits you did or if you were surprised by each others choices:

_____
_____
_____
_____
_____
_____
_____
_____
_____
_____
_____
_____
_____
_____
_____
_____
_____
_____

Congratulations

You are now the
Supreme Ruler of Earth
and you may solve one world problem
today. What will it be?

_____   Disease

_____   War & Terrorism

_____   Climate Change & Pollution

_____   Poverty & Starvation

_____   Drug & Substance Abuse

Place a check mark on the right to predict
your daughters choice.

Congratulations

You are now the
Supreme Ruler of Earth
and you may solve one world problem
today. What will it be?

_____ Disease

_____ War & Terrorism

_____ Climate Change & Pollution

_____ Poverty & Starvation

_____ Drug & Substance Abuse

Place a check mark on the right to predict your dads choice.

We answer/discuss

After you both have answered, discuss or write why you made the choice you did. What would have been your second choices?

_____
_____
_____
_____
_____
_____
_____
_____
_____
_____
_____
_____
_____
_____
_____
_____
_____
_____

When you were little where was the scariest place in your room?

_ _ _ _ _ _   Under the bed

_ _ _ _ _ _   In the closet

_ _ _ _ _ _   Outside the window

_ _ _ _ _ _   Somewhere else?

What did you think was hiding? What did you think would happen?

_____

_____

_____

_____

_____

_____

_____

_____

When you were little where was the scariest place in your room?

_____ Under the bed

_____ In the closet

_____ Outside the window

_____ Somewhere else?

What did you think was hiding? What did you think would happen?

_____
_____
_____
_____
_____
_____
_____
_____
_____
_____

Did you tell anyone about your fears? Do you still fear something in your room sometimes? Dad, tell or write about a time when your daughter was scared.

_____

_____

_____

_____

_____

_____

_____

_____

_____

_____

_____

_____

_____

_____

_____

_____

_____

What 2 things are you the most worried about regarding your daughter right now?

_____

_____

What 2 things are you the most worried about regarding your daughter in the future?

_____

_____

Name one thing in your daughters life that you think she is the most worried about right now:

_____

Who worries more about her life? (circle one)

I do   She does

What 2 things in your life are you the most worried about right now?

_____

_____

What 2 things in your life are you the most worried about in your future?

_____

_____

Name one thing in your dads life that you think he is the most worried about right now:

_____

Who worries the most about your life? (circle one)

I do   He does

We answer/discuss

Is there anything you can do about the things you're worried about? Is there anything you can do for each other?

_____

_____

_____

_____

_____

_____

_____

_____

_____

_____

_____

_____

_____

_____

_____

_____

Dad answer

About School....
This year what subject does your daughter...

do the best in?

_____

like the most?

_____

like the least?

_____

find the easiest?

_____

find the hardest?

_____

What subject can you help her the most in? The least in?

_____

_____

_____

_____

_____

About School....
This year what subject do you...

do the best in?

_____

like the most?

_____

like the least?

_____

find the easiest?

_____

find the hardest?

_____

What subject can your dad help you the most in?
The least in?

_____

_____

_____

_____

_____

We answer/discuss

Were you surprised by each other's choices?
Dad, share what was hardest and easiest for you
in school.

_____

_____

_____

_____

_____

_____

_____

_____

_____

_____

_____

_____

_____

_____

_____

_____

_____

_____

Do you believe in ghosts?
yes / no

Why or why not?

_____

_____

_____

_____

Does your daughter believe in ghosts?
yes/no

◇◇◇◇◇◇◇◇◇◇◇◇◇◇◇◇◇◇◇◇◇◇◇◇◇◇◇◇◇◇◇◇

Do you believe in aliens?
yes / no

Why or why not?

_____

_____

_____

_____

Does your daughter believe in aliens?
yes/no

Do you believe in ghosts?
yes / no

Why or why not?

_____

_____

_____

_____

Does your dad believe in ghosts?
yes/no

Do you believe in aliens?
yes / no

Why or why not?

_____

_____

_____

_____

Does your dad believe in aliens?
yes/no

Have you ever or do you know someone who has had a personal experience with either? Did you believe them? Which one do you hope exists more?

_____

_____

_____

_____

_____

_____

_____

_____

_____

_____

_____

_____

_____

_____

_____

_____

_____

_____

Dad answer

What two things have you taught your daughter?

_____

_____

_____

_____

What two things have you learned from your daughter?

_____

_____

_____

_____

What are two things you could teach your dad?

_____

_____

_____

_____

What are the two best things you have learned from your dad?

_____

_____

_____

_____

We answer/discuss

Come up with at least one thing it would be fun for both of you to learn together.

_____

_____

_____

_____

_____

_____

_____

_____

_____

_____

_____

_____

_____

_____

_____

_____

_____

You're throwing a party for your daughter next weekend. Rank what you think her top three choices would be:

	Sleep over
	Surprise party
	Costume party
	Game night
	Cooking party
	Sing/Dance party
	Pool party (indoor)
	Spa party

You're getting a party next weekend!
Rank what your top three choices
would be:

	Sleep over
	Surprise party
	Costume party
	Game night
	Cooking party
	Sing/Dance party
	Pool party (indoor)
	Spa party

Dad, what kind of parties did you have or attend at your daughters age?

_____

_____

_____

_____

_____

_____

_____

_____

_____

_____

_____

_____

_____

_____

_____

_____

_____

_____

What 3 positive traits would describe your daughter?

_____

_____

_____

What are 2 things she does that you appreciate?

_____

_____

Daughter answer

What 3 positive traits would describe your dad?

_____

_____

_____

What are 2 things he does that you appreciate?

_____

_____

Did your dad/daughter know what you appreciated about him/her?

_____

_____

_____

_____

_____

_____

_____

_____

_____

_____

_____

_____

_____

_____

_____

_____

_____

_____

Check 3 things you'd like to do more of with your daughter:

_____ cook together

_____ play games

_____ have conversations

_____ be active (sports/walks/bike rides...)

_____ go out to lunch or dinner

_____ watch TV

_____ play video games

_____ do crafts/art/projects

_____ _____

Check 3 things you'd like to do more of with your dad:

_____ cook together

_____ play games

_____ have conversations

_____ be active (sports/walks/bike rides...)

_____ go out to lunch or dinner

_____ watch TV

_____ play video games

_____ do crafts/art/projects

_____ _____

We answer/discuss

After you both have answered, agree to do at least one that you both checked sometime in the next week or two.

_____

_____

_____

_____

_____

_____

_____

_____

_____

_____

_____

_____

_____

_____

_____

_____

_____

_____

Hola! Bonjour! Ciao!
Namaste! Salaam!
Ni Hau! Ola! Bula!

You woke up this morning fluent in a new language. What do you hope it is?

_____

Why?

_____

_____

_____

What would you want it to be for your daughter?

_____

Why?

_____

_____

Hola! Bonjour! Ciao!
Namaste! Salaam!
Ni Hau! Ola! Bula!

You woke up this morning fluent in a new language. What do you hope it is?

_____

Why?

_____

_____

_____

What would you want it to be for your dad?

_____

Why?

_____

_____

We answer/discuss

What do you think would make the best common world language that everyone would learn as a child?

_____

_____

_____

_____

_____

_____

_____

_____

_____

_____

_____

_____

_____

_____

_____

_____

_____

Do you think your daughter has ever...

	yes	no
Eaten a bug?		
Been in a physical fight?		
Been bullied?		
Had a crush?		
Lied about her age?		
Stayed up all night?		
Seen something illegal?		
Sent an e-mail or text by mistake?		
Hid something from you?		
Gotten away with something at school?		
Made a prank phone call?		

When you're both done, check the ones on her side that are correct about you.

Daughter answer

Do you think your dad has ever...

	yes	no
Eaten a bug?		
Been in a physical fight?		
Been bullied?		
Had a crush?		
Lied about his age?		
Stayed up all night?		
Seen something illegal?		
Sent an e-mail or text by mistake?		
Hid something from you?		
Gotten away with something at school?		
Made a prank phone call?		

When you're both done, check the ones on his side that are correct about you.

List 3 things you are proud of your daughter for this year:

_____

_____

_____

List 2 things you are proud of yourself for this year:

_____

_____

_____

List 3 things you are proud of yourself for this year:

_____

_____

_____

List 1 thing you are proud of your dad for this year:

_____

_____

_____

We answer/discuss

Was is hard or easy to come up with these? What is one thing you wish you could add to your list?

_____

_____

_____

_____

_____

_____

_____

_____

_____

_____

_____

_____

_____

_____

_____

_____

_____

_____

In your ideal job/career what are the top three things that are most important for you?

_____ Great location

_____ Rewarding/love it

_____ Lots of travel

_____ High income

_____ Great co-workers

_____ Lots of time off

_____ Be my own boss

_____ Makes a difference

Place a check next to the two you think your daughter will choose.

In your ideal job/career what are the top three things that will be the most important for you?

_____ Great location

_____ Rewarding/love it

_____ Lots of travel

_____ High income

_____ Great co-workers

_____ Lots of time off

_____ Be my own boss

_____ Makes a difference

Place a check next to the two you think your dad will choose.

We answer/discuss

Dad, have you achieved the things you chose? Have they changed over time?

_____
_____
_____
_____
_____
_____
_____
_____
_____
_____
_____
_____
_____
_____
_____
_____
_____
_____
_____
_____
_____

Dad answer

What are two ways you still treat your daughter like a little kid?

_____

_____

What are two ways you treat her like an adult?

_____

_____

Daughter answer

Read what your Dad wrote. Check the ones you agree with. If you want to add different things put them below:

_____

_____

_____

In what way do you wish your dad would treat you more like an adult? (communication, responsibility, trust?)

_____

_____

_____

We answer/discuss

Discuss what you think are reasonable ways to work out disagreements with each other.

_____

_____

_____

_____

_____

_____

_____

_____

_____

_____

_____

_____

_____

_____

_____

_____

_____

_____

Dad answer

What do you think is better of the choices below?

	Winning $20	Finding $20	
	City	Country	
	Surprises	Planned events	
	Extra Credit	Curve	
	Running	Swimming	
	Spring	Fall	

What do you think your daughter will choose?

	Winning $20	Finding $20	
	City	Country	
	Surprises	Planned events	
	Extra Credit	Curve	
	Running	Swimming	
	Spring	Fall	

What do you think is better of the choices below?

	Winning $20	Finding $20	
	City	Country	
	Surprises	Planned events	
	Extra Credit	Curve	
	Running	Swimming	
	Spring	Fall	

What do you think your dad will choose?

	Winning $20	Finding $20	
	City	Country	
	Surprises	Planned events	
	Extra Credit	Curve	
	Running	Swimming	
	Spring	Fall	

We answer/discuss

If you found a suitcase full of money in the woods, what would you do? What if it contained $50, $500, or $50,000?

_____

_____

_____

_____

_____

_____

_____

_____

_____

_____

_____

_____

_____

_____

_____

_____

_____

Circle the three life goals that you wish most for your daughter. Place a check next to the ones you've done or are doing:

Being healthy

Having a successful career

Caring for others

Making the world a better place

Having a life partner

Being rich

Having children

Being happy

Having close friends

Being famous

Exploring/Traveling

Circle the three life goals that you wish most for yourself.

Being healthy

Having a successful career

Caring for others

Making the world a better place

Having a life partner

Being rich

Having children

Being happy

Having close friends

Being famous

Exploring/Traveling

We answer/discuss

Dad, how have your priorities changed over time? Daughter, how do you think your priorities will change over time?

_____

_____

_____

_____

_____

_____

_____

_____

_____

_____

_____

_____

_____

_____

_____

_____

_____

Which 3 qualities do you think your daughter needs most from you?

Encouragement	
Clear and consistent rules	
A sense of humor	
Listening without giving advice	
Genuine interest in activities	
Direction and guidance	
Setting a good example	
Open communication	
Unconditional love	
Understanding and forgiveness	

Pick the top 2 qualities you need most from your dad:

Encouragement	
Clear and consistent rules	
A sense of humor	
Listening without giving advice	
Genuine interest in activities	
Direction and guidance	
Setting a good example	
Open communication	
Unconditional love	
Understanding and forgiveness	

We answer/discuss

Discuss or write about one area that you could really use more support in from your dad:

_____

_____

_____

_____

_____

_____

_____

_____

_____

_____

_____

_____

_____

_____

_____

_____

_____

Do you believe in miracles?
yes / no

Why or why not?

_____

_____

_____

_____

Does your daughter believe in miracles?
yes / no

◇◇◇◇◇◇◇◇◇◇◇◇◇◇◇◇◇◇◇◇◇◇◇◇◇◇◇◇◇◇◇◇

Do you believe in guardian angels?
yes / no

Why or why not?

_____

_____

_____

_____

Does your daughter believe in guardian angels?
yes / no

Do you believe in miracles?
yes / no

Why or why not?

_____

_____

_____

_____

Does your dad believe in miracles?
yes / no

◇◇◇◇◇◇◇◇◇◇◇◇◇◇◇◇◇◇◇◇◇◇◇◇◇◇◇◇◇◇◇

Do you believe in guardian angels?
yes / no

Why or why not?

_____

_____

_____

_____

Does your dad believe in guardian angels?
yes / no

We answer/discuss

Have you ever or do you know someone who has had a personal experience with either? Did you believe them? Which one do you hope exists more?

_____

_____

_____

_____

_____

_____

_____

_____

_____

_____

_____

_____

_____

_____

_____

_____

_____

_____

Your daughter will be living in one of these for the summer. Which will be her top two choices?

What would be your top three choices?

	Her	Me
an RV		
a yurt		
a tiny house		
a deluxe tree house		
a sailboat		
a tent		
a houseboat		

Daughter answer

You will be living in one of these for the summer. Which are your top three choices?

What would be your dads top two choices?

	Me	Him
an RV		
a yurt		
a tiny house		
a deluxe tree house		
a sailboat		
a tent		
a houseboat		

We answer/discuss

Which one of you deals better with change? Is the idea of living in a different place exciting or stressful?

_____
_____
_____
_____
_____
_____
_____
_____
_____
_____
_____
_____
_____
_____
_____
_____
_____
_____
_____

Dad answer

What are 2 things you think you have done right in raising your daughter?

_____

_____

_____

_____

What is something you wish you had done better or different in raising your daughter?

_____

_____

_____

_____

What is one thing you could still improve on?

_____

_____

_____

_____

Read what your dad has written.

Place check marks next to the ones you agree with.

Place X's next to the ones you don't agree with.

What is one thing you will do the same in raising your children?

_____

_____

_____

_____

What is one thing you will do different in raising your children?

_____

_____

_____

_____

We answer/discuss

Dad, what is a difference between the way you were treated as a child and the way you have treated her.

_____

_____

_____

_____

_____

_____

_____

_____

_____

_____

_____

_____

_____

_____

_____

_____

_____

_____

Dad answer

In what two ways are you and your daughter the most alike?

_____

_____

_____

_____

In what two ways are you and your daughter the most different?

_____

_____

_____

_____

Daughter answer

In what two ways are you and your dad the most alike?

_____

_____

_____

_____

In what two ways are you and your dad the most different?

_____

_____

_____

_____

We answer/discuss

Do you work better together as a team or is it better if you divide and attack tasks separately? At school/work do you prefer working by yourself or in a group?

_____

_____

_____

_____

_____

_____

_____

_____

_____

_____

_____

_____

_____

_____

_____

_____

_____

_____

Dad answer

Which of you .... more?

	Dad	Daughter
daydreams		
complains		
relaxes		
is in the bathroom		
finds happiness in little things		
judges other people		
gives advice		
communicates		
has fun		

Daughter answer

Which of you .... more?

	Me	You
dreams		
complains		
relaxes		
is in the bathroom		
finds happiness in little things		
judges other people		
gives advice		
communicates		
has fun		

We answer/discuss

Did you agree? Which would be good for both
of you to do more of? Less of?

_____

_____

_____

_____

_____

_____

_____

_____

_____

_____

_____

_____

_____

_____

_____

_____

_____

_____

So...it turns out you get a super power on your next birthday that will last exactly one month. What do you hope it is?

____ mind control

____ invisibility

____ super strength & speed

____ ability to fly

____ healing

How will you use it?

_____

_____

_____

What will your daughter choose?

____ mind control   ____ invisibility

____ super strength & speed

____ ability to fly   ____ healing

91

So...it turns out you get a super power on your next birthday that will last exactly one month. What do you hope it is?

_____ mind control

_____ invisibility

_____ super strength & speed

_____ ability to fly

_____ healing

How will you use it?

_____

_____

_____

What will your dad choose?

_____ mind control   _____ invisibility

_____ super strength & speed

_____ ability to fly   _____ healing

92

What if you got to keep the power, but it would shorten your life by 10 years. Would it be worth it? If everyone in the world had one of these powers what would be the best choice for all?

_____

_____

_____

_____

_____

_____

_____

_____

_____

_____

_____

_____

_____

_____

_____

_____

Do you believe in karma?
yes / no

Why or why not?

_____

_____

_____

_____

Does your daughter believe in karma?
yes/no

◇◇◇◇◇◇◇◇◇◇◇◇◇◇◇◇◇◇◇◇◇◇◇◇◇◇◇◇◇◇◇

Do you believe in love at first sight?
yes / no

Why or why not?

_____

_____

_____

_____

Does your daughter believe in love at
first sight?
yes/no

95

Daughter answer

Do you believe in karma?
yes / no

Why or why not?

_____

_____

_____

_____

Does your dad believe in karma?
yes/no

Do you believe in love at first sight?
yes / no

Why or why not?

_____

_____

_____

_____

Does your dad believe in love at first sight?
yes/no

We answer/discuss

Have you ever or do you know someone who has had a personal experience with either? Did you believe them? Which one do you hope exists more?

_____
_____
_____
_____
_____
_____
_____
_____
_____
_____
_____
_____
_____
_____
_____
_____
_____

Dad answer

You just won a time travel trip!

Do you want to go:

_____ to the past

_____ to the future

what period of time in the past or how far into the future?

_____

_____

What would you want to see or do?

_____

_____

Do you think your daughter will want to go:

_____ to the past

_____ to the future

You just won a time travel trip!

Do you want to go:

_____ to the past

_____ to the future

what period of time in the past or how far into the future?

_____

_____

What would you want to see or do?

_____

_____

Do you think your dad will want to go:

_____ to the past

_____ to the future

100

Who would you want to meet? Where would you like to go together? If you had to be there permantently, would you make the same choice?

_____

_____

_____

_____

_____

_____

_____

_____

_____

_____

_____

_____

_____

_____

_____

_____

_____

Your daughter just won a **Vacation Home** that she can use every weekend. The perfect place would be...(check one in each group)

located

_____ on the oceanfront

_____ in the mountains

_____ by a lake

with a great view of the

_____ sunrise

_____ sunset

There would be plenty of

_____ outdoor activities

_____ indoor activities

and lots of

_____ quiet time

_____ parties

You just won a **Vacation Home** that you can use every weekend. The perfect place would be...(check one in each group)

located

_____   on the oceanfront

_____   in the mountains

_____   by a lake

with a great view of the

_____   sunrise

_____   sunset

There would be plenty of

_____   outdoor activities

_____   indoor activities

and lots of

_____   quiet time

_____   parties

Would you want to live there permanently? Why or why not?

_____

_____

_____

_____

_____

_____

_____

_____

_____

_____

_____

_____

_____

_____

_____

_____

_____

Dad – *draw your daughters favorite*

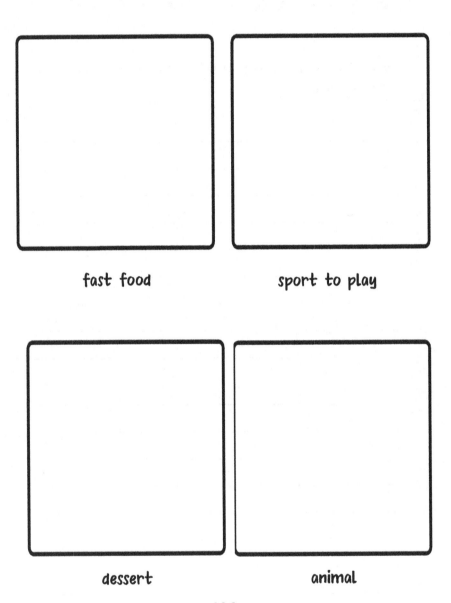

fast food

sport to play

dessert

animal

Daughter – draw your dads favorite

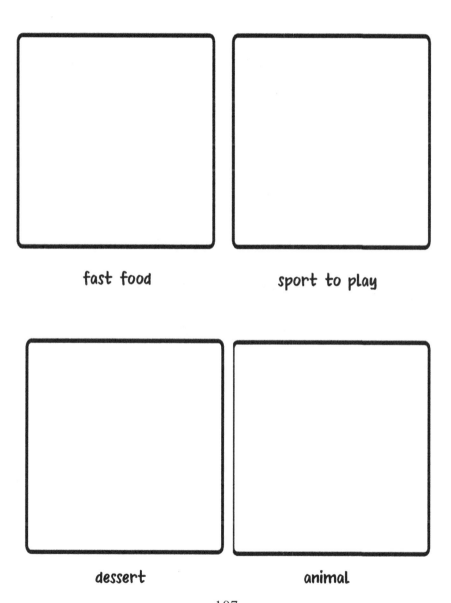

fast food

sport to play

dessert

animal

Check 3 things you hope your daughter knows:

_____ how much I love her

_____ what a great person I think she is

_____ how much I worry about her

_____ how much I believe in her

_____ how much I trust her

_____ how special she is

_____ how much I expect of her

Daughter answer

Check 3 things you hope your dad knows:

_____ that I'm trying

_____ that there are a lot of pressures on me

_____ that I know he want the best for me

_____ that he can trust me

_____ that I'm not going to do anything really stupid

_____ that I need space to grow

_____ that I think about my future

Dad answer

Question:

_____

_____

_____

Answer:

_____

_____

_____

_____

_____

_____

_____

_____

_____

_____

_____

_____

_____

_____

_____

Daughter answer

Question:

_____

_____

_____

Answer:

_____

_____

_____

_____

_____

_____

_____

_____

_____

_____

_____

_____

_____

_____

_____

_____

Dad answer

Question:

_____

_____

_____

Answer:

_____

_____

_____

_____

_____

_____

_____

_____

_____

_____

_____

_____

_____

_____

_____

Daughter answer

Question:

_____

_____

_____

Answer:

_____

_____

_____

_____

_____

_____

_____

_____

_____

_____

_____

_____

_____

_____

_____

_____

_____

Dad answer

Question:

_____

_____

_____

Answer:

_____

_____

_____

_____

_____

_____

_____

_____

_____

_____

_____

_____

_____

_____

_____

_____

_____

Daughter answer

Question:

_____

_____

_____

Answer:

_____

_____

_____

_____

_____

_____

_____

_____

_____

_____

_____

_____

_____

_____

_____

_____

Dad answer

Question:

_____

_____

_____

Answer:

_____

_____

_____

_____

_____

_____

_____

_____

_____

_____

_____

_____

_____

_____

_____

_____

_____

Daughter answer

Question:

_____

_____

_____

Answer:

_____

_____

_____

_____

_____

_____

_____

_____

_____

_____

_____

_____

_____

_____

_____

Dad answer

Question:

_____

_____

_____

Answer:

_____

_____

_____

_____

_____

_____

_____

_____

_____

_____

_____

_____

_____

_____

Daughter answer

Question:

_____

_____

_____

Answer:

_____

_____

_____

_____

_____

_____

_____

_____

_____

_____

_____

_____

_____

_____

_____

_____

Dad answer

Question:

_____

_____

_____

Answer:

_____

_____

_____

_____

_____

_____

_____

_____

_____

_____

_____

_____

_____

_____

_____

_____

Daughter answer

Question:

_____

_____

_____

Answer:

_____

_____

_____

_____

_____

_____

_____

_____

_____

_____

_____

_____

_____

_____

Dad answer

Question:

_____

_____

_____

Answer:

_____

_____

_____

_____

_____

_____

_____

_____

_____

_____

_____

_____

_____

_____

_____

_____

Daughter answer

Question:

_____

_____

_____

Answer:

_____

_____

_____

_____

_____

_____

_____

_____

_____

_____

_____

_____

_____

_____

Made in the USA
Las Vegas, NV
21 December 2023

83353597R00075